# How to make a batch of resilience

## Merryl Semple
### Illustrated by Marieke Nelissen

Take a jolt of adrenaline
A half measure of attention
Surge with negative emotion

If it binds up, chokes or steams
Sinks or slumps
Has any fractious reactions

Soak in an ease of breath

You may need two
or three

Be alert to the temperature
Watch for lingering bubbles of defensiveness
Continue to apply an ease of breaths

Until

You can stir the fullness of awareness rising
The warm spread of inner ease

Sprinkle your gaze with soft curiosity
Gel your hearing with possibility
Handle the batch with positive intention

Dose freely with appreciation
It creates the right conditions

Watch with humble grace and wonder
The batch of resilience maturing
Continuously baste with acceptance and gratitude

Gently fold in the light expansion of perspective
Rest in the heart of understanding and compassion

Then share.

## Notes to the Cook

It is enough as a first step, to soak in the ease of breath. This alone will stop your batch from overcooking.

If you are mean with appreciation, your batch will be prone to fermentation and sourness.

Each successful batch becomes resilient to contamination from master chefs who focus on winning.

Each last batch will be lighter, more nourishing and you will experience spontaneous bubbles of kindness and delight.

Make it a staple on your daily menu.

How to Make a Batch of Resilience
Author – Merryl Semple

Text Copyright © Merryl Semple 2020
Illustration Copyright © Marieke Nelissen 2020

This book is sold with the understanding that the author is not offering specific personal advice to the reader. For professional advice, seek the services of a suitable, qualified practitioner. The author disclaims any responsibility for liability, loss or risk, personal or otherwise, that happens as a consequence of the use and application of any of the contents of this book.

All rights reserved. This book may not be reproduced in whole or part, stored, posted on the internet, or transmitted in any form or by any means, electronic, mechanical, photocopying, recording, or other, without permission from the author of this book.

ISBN: 978-0-6450551-0-8

A catalogue record for this book is available from the National Library of Australia

www.ingramcontent.com/pod-product-compliance
Lightning Source LLC
Chambersburg PA
CBHW041156290426
44108CB00002B/86